A Manual for Stewardship Development Programs in the Congregation

Edited by Thomas R. Gossen,
Executive Director of The Episcopal Network for Stewardship

with significant contributions by sustaining members of The Episcopal Network for Stewardship

Morehouse Publishing
4775 Linglestown Road
Harrisburg, PA 17112

Morehouse Publishing is an imprint of Church Publishing Incorporated.

ISBN 10: 0-8192-1679-8
ISBN 13: 978-0-8192-1679-3

Printed in the United States of America

Table of Contents

Preface to Second Edition

by The Rev. J. Hugh Magers

I have been actively involved in stewardship ministries in the Episcopal Church during more than 30 years as a parish priest, a diocesan ecclesiocrat, and a national officer for both stewardship and evangelism. During that time, I have become ever more convinced of the validity of the following seven truths concerning financial development programs in the church, in particular, and stewardship development programs, in general.

1. The first place to look for money is in the heart, not the wallet. In my experience, about 75% of the annual income of the typical congregation comes from 12 to 15% of the members. These folks also do most of the ministry of the church. They usually can talk about the ways that they have known God in their lives. The amount of giving is not connected to the amount of money that they have. There are rich and poor, stingy people. Generous people come in all economic categories. The key to stimulating the primary givers is to keep a steady supply of stories of lives saved and changed by the Gospel of Jesus Christ. That means that the Gospel is being preached, taught, lived, and that peoples' lives are being changed.

2. Most people find it hard to talk about God and money. God and money are both wonderful and powerful. Most people are so afraid of them that they can't talk about them. So we need to create arenas where it is safe to do so. I have found that small groups and studying the Bible can, with prayer and over time, talk about God and money. I have also found that unless this conversation takes place, there will be no basic change in giving patterns.

3. Though it stirs folks up, we still have to talk about the tithe. God has every right to require the tithe. I see no mention in Holy Scripture of God asking us what we think about it. The irony is that most folk who submit themselves to that discipline find it to be a rewarding and uplifting practice. I have a friend who says: "God and I can do together more with 90% of my money than I can do on my own with 100%." I personally don't believe that God blesses those who tithe in special ways. But while I don't believe it, my experience confirms it. The word "tithe" occurs 67 times in the Scriptures. Indeed, about one-third of Jesus' parables deal with money. In fact, Jesus makes reference to the tithe in Matthew 23:23 in a most powerful way. If someone wants to fight the tithe, they have to fight the Bible.

4. We aren't saved because we give money to God. Salvation is a gift from God's grace that comes through faith (itself a gift from God). We enter life in grace through our Baptisms and our claiming of Jesus as Savior and our submission to his Lordship. We grow in grace through steady participation in worship and ministry. Giving will not affect your salvation. Salvation will definitely affect your giving.

5. Everyone is already doing the very best they can. Everyone is already giving everything they can, given their spiritual health. In fact, your giving rate is a pretty good indicator of your spiritual health. Whatever you give, give it with joy. The difference between what you give and what God wants you to give is made up by Jesus in the same way that Jesus bridges our sinfulness and God's holiness.

6. Yes, we really do need to sign pledge cards. At one level, a pledge card is merely an act of kindness to the vestry and treasurer since it enables them to plan a budget. But at a deeper level, people who pledge feel like they belong to the Church. So pledging is an identity or community statement. At the deepest level, a pledge card is the only document that most of us sign every year saying that we claim Jesus as Savior and submit our lives to his Lordship.

7. If you are not smiling when you sign your pledge card, you have filled in the wrong amount. You have pledged too much or too little. Give a happy amount!

How we bring these truths into the culture and common practice in our congregations will vary. Some will be more successful than others. *A Manual for Stewardship Development Programs in the Congregation* can be of invaluable assistance. Much of the content of this manual is material that has accumulated over 15+ years of practical experience throughout the Church. I am delighted that The Episcopal Network for Stewardship, Inc. (TENS), together with our publishing partner, Morehouse Publishing, is taking a leadership role in continuing to make this material available. TENS emerged out of an enthusiasm for wanting to continue a consistent, quality ministry with those called to lead stewardship programs in their parish and diocese to become an important resource for the Church. TENS is a membership organization and everyone's participation is encouraged. I am pleased to commend *A Manual for Stewardship Development Programs in the Congregation* (and the accompanying five workbooks) to your attention and use.

Foreword to Second Edition

by
Tom Gossen

"*The point is this: the one who sows sparingly will also reap sparingly, and the one who sows bountifully will also reap bountifully. Each of your must give as you have made up your mind, not reluctantly or under compulsion, for God loves a cheerful giver. And God is able to provide you with every blessing in abundance, so that by always having enough of everything, you may share abundantly in every good work.*"
2 Corinthians 9:6-8 (NRSV)

This passage from second Corinthians challenges me every time I pause to reflect on its message. I certainly know that there have been, and continue to be, times when I give reluctantly. And, I know that when I make my own gift to the annual appeal for The Episcopal Network for Stewardship, I certainly give with some sense of compulsion—I have to give as the leader of the organization! Paul's message suggests that we should independently make up our minds and be cheerful about it!

As a giver, I have discovered that it's not so much what I discern in my mind that governs my decision on the amount that I will give, but rather my emotional (or heartfelt) ties with the organization to which I am contributing. "If my heart's not in it" there will be little to be cheerful (or joyful) about and, the organization will have difficulty in realizing a gift. I believe that's true for most (if not all) of us—if our heart's not in it, there will be little or no gift.

The opportunity then, is to discover ways to grow grateful and generous hearts for the spread of God's Kingdom. The challenge, however, might best be illustrated by the conversation I once had with The Rt. Rev. Richard Grein who advised me that "we don't have money problems in the Church, we have belief problems. If everyone only truly believed what they recite in their Baptismal Covenant and what they recite every Sunday in the Creed, we would have no lack of money. We would, however, be challenged by an overabundance of enthusiastic Christians that would need to be placed in meaningful ministries."

In my experience, growing Joyful Givers can only be accomplished one heart at a time. There is no single formula, or program, that works for everyone. It is possible, however, to begin to make significant changes in the culture of a congregation when the clergy and lay leadership are seriously committed to the challenge and willing to invest the time and energy by beginning with examining their own beliefs and practices and then inviting the congregation to join them. In some cases, the lay leadership chosen to begin with may not be the elected vestry (or council), because the message would not fall on receptive ears. It is my prayer that this resource and the accompanying workbooks might continue to offer assistance to those who wish to take seriously the ministry of stewardship formation in their congregation.

I am delighted that the first edition of *A Manual for Stewardship Development Programs in the Congregation* was accepted with enough enthusiasm to warrant the printing of a second edition. When the first edition was assembled in 1996, we were working with a great sense of urgency to produce a usable how-to manual for leaders in congregations. I would like to think that this edition has been prepared more leisurely; however, when I approach anything leisurely, it never seems to quite reach completion. So I am certain that with this edition, as with the first, there are topics that could use expansion, and subjects not addressed that should have been.

At the risk of offending someone by not mentioning them, I am compelled to express my gratitude and sincere thanks to the many individuals who have had a significant impact on my spiritual journey, in general, and my journey in stewardship, in particular.

To my spouse Diane, who reflects my words and deeds to me in ways that help to clarify if I'm really saying and living what I hope to profess. Diane patiently endures the time I spend dedicated to many "worthy projects." Becoming a parent and grandparent with Diane has truly been one of life's greatest joys.

To Ann Elizabeth Bishop who recruited me to serve on the diocesan stewardship commission and who coordinated a visit by The Rev. Robert Bonner to Wichita to present a workshop that was the beginning of many wonderful changes for me and many of my fellow parishioners at St. Alban's, Wichita.

To my (former) priest and dear friend, Sam Criss, who tolerated my frequent offerings of advice and whose insight and thoughtful processing of ideas with me has been, and continues to be, most helpful.

To The Rev. Ron Reed who has become a dear kindred spirit while serving as rector of St. James, Wichita. As former director of the Office of Stewardship at the Episcopal Church Center, Ron brings the knowledge of many years of practical experience and a passion for teaching stewardship theology.

To Bruce Rockwell, whose life was significantly impacted by the ministry of The Rev. Tom Carson and The Rev. Ron Reed, and who continues to model for me how laity can realize an effective ministry.

To The Rev. J. Hugh Magers, who exemplifies for me everything it means to be an Evangelical, and who took a chance in hiring me to serve as a Field Officer for the Office of Stewardship while he was Staff Officer for Stewardship. I am grateful that Hugh continues to challenge me to climb higher and to reach farther in leading the ministry of TENS.

To The Rev. William A. (Bill) Yon of the Diocese of Alabama, who was instrumental (along with others) in analyzing and focusing attention on the conditions in congregational life that affect stewardship formation. From this work came a program known throughout the Episcopal Church as "the Alabama Plan."

To Terry Parsons, who now leads the Stewardship Program at the

Episcopal Church Center, and who continues to amaze me with her energy, enthusiasm and belief that we truly can make a difference when we accept God's abundance and begin to live into it.

To The Very Rev. Robert Giannini, Dean of Christ Church Cathedral, Indianapolis and the members of the Outreach Committee who caught the vision of the importance of an independent national ministry and who provided crucial funding to underwrite the creation of TENS and its on-going ministry.

And, to the many countless others who have, and who continue to contribute to the ministry of The Episcopal Network for Stewardship through your sharing of yourselves through the offerings of advice and counsel, sharing materials developed in your congregation and diocese, and sharing of your material wealth.

Thank you!

The first edition has a by line that suggests that Lonnie Schreiber and I authored the material, when in reality, we assembled content that had proven useful over a number of years from various practitioners and presented it, along with our own thoughts, in a hopefully useable format. Lonnie, who remains a dear friend, is no longer active in stewardship ministries. While active, she was faithful and did a wonderful job. Multiple Sclerosis has taken its toll on her abilities, thought she still functions abundantly well as a grandmother. She assures me that her prayers continue to be with all of us as we work in the vineyard of stewardship ministries. I extend to her a special thanks for her friendship and council and for her many years of dedicated service to the ministry of stewardship development in the Episcopal Church.

 Tom Gossen, a retired Architect, has served as the Executive Director for The Episcopal Network for Stewardship (TENS) since 1995. He has extensive experience in leading and developing programs for dioceses and congregations, including the training of consultants/mentors. Publications include *A Manual for Stewardship Development Programs in the Congregation* and five different commitment program workbooks published by Morehouse Publishing. Tom was chairperson of the Diocese of Kansas Commission on Stewardship and Development for 12 years and served a six-year term on the Episcopal Church's Standing Commission on Stewardship and Development. He currently is serving a six-year term as a member of the Executive Council of the Episcopal Church from 2003–2009.

Tom and his wife, Diane, have two grown children and two grandchildren, Jacob and Katherine Pennington.

Education for
Stewardship
Development

Purpose

The purpose of this manual, and the accompanying workbooks, is to provide resources to congregational leaders in the timeless teachings of Christian Stewardship and to provide some practical applications of these teachings.

Stewardship Development (or Formation) Programs are those things that we do throughout the church year to educate one another in what it means...

■ to accept Jesus as our Lord and Savior, and

■ to invite one another to make a personal commitment to offer thanks for all of our blessings and to support God's work in the world.

We use a formula: E + CP = SDP

E is for Education

CP is for Commitment Program

SDP is for Stewardship Development Program

If a congregation does only a Commitment (or pledge) Program without the ongoing Education, the Stewardship Development Program will fail to fund God's mission for the congregation. It is imperative to do both Education and Commitment Programs. A Commitment Program with little or no Education will not give the congregation an opportunity to focus on the reality of God's loving forgiveness and grace. Once people have begun to understand and embrace God's unconditional love and grace, funding the mission of the Church becomes a joy and is no longer a chore. Also, the failure to have a Commitment Program means that any superb Education will have few mission consequences. It is imperative to include both an Education and a Commitment Program.

To achieve maximum effectiveness, Stewardship Education must be a year-round program. Some formal teaching is done every month in a year-round program. It may come in a task, a sermon, an adult education effort, monthly newsletters and weekly bulletins. There are resources available for children and adult Sunday School programs as well.

Many topics are reviewed or taught under the heading of Stewardship. One of the purposes of those assigned the ministry of the Stewardship Development Program is to provide year-round teaching to broaden the definition of stewardship so that the words "stewardship" and "tithe" are not first mentioned in October or November in the context of the annual pledge drive. When people are not surprised that sharing of our most precious resources for the spread of God's Kingdom is an act of Stewardship, then good teaching is evident. There are many other signs of sound education. This manual identifies some of them.

1. Action Date. A fixed date for each part of the program (i.e. by July 9, we will have recruited 10 homes and hosts for our Cottage Meeting Commitment Program).

2. Action Plan. Action Plans are a resource to help a congregation act out their Mission Statement. The process of creating Action Plans generates energy and enthusiasm for ministry among the participants in the Action Plan workshops. Action Plans are blueprints to guide the building of specific ministries out of that energy and enthusiasm. Action Plans inform people how and where their money will go if they decide to give more.

> "Vision without love-impelled action should always be suspect."
> Evelyn Underhill. "The Authority of Personal Religious
> Experience." Theology. Vol. X, No. 55, 1925, pp. 8-24

3. Annual Giving. The essential giving that supports the mission of the church. Approximately 90% of the income of the church comes from the annual financial commitments of the members.

4. Biblical Stewardship. We look to the Bible for the nucleus of all Stewardship teaching and practice. All the issues and concerns of Stewardship: money, time, energy, skill, relationships, the environment, and the institutional church are established somewhere in the Bible. All teaching must begin with scripture.

5. Capital Giving. These are offerings (often from accumulated assets of the giver) that build and/or maintain the resources used in mission and ministry. Usually these are physical resources.

6. Conversion and Repentance. In the New Testament there are two Greek words that are translated as conversion and repentance. They are Epistrophe and Metanoia. Epistrophe means turning point and it has to do with our behavior. It parallels St. Paul's understanding of sin as missing the mark. Metanoia means coming to wholeness of mind. It is the opposite of paranoia. Both meanings are essential in Stewardship behavior. The purpose of conversion is to increase our capacity to see God.

7. Giver of Record. These are the people who give to the church in a way that enables the Treasurer to keep a record of their giving. Almost all givers of record make a written financial commitment or pledge and then fulfill it with their regular offerings. Some prefer to not make an annual pledge, but do give by check or in an envelope.

8. Inductive Bible Study. This method of Bible study is not scholarly but devotional. It relies on God speaking to the believer through the scripture. There are several methods of Inductive Bible Study. All effective Stewardship Education begins with Inductive Bible Study. All Stewardship Education seeks to invite the participants into a deeper understanding of their relationship with their Lord and Savior, Jesus Christ.

A Glossary of Stewardship Terms and Phrases

9. Line Item Budget. This is a budget format to identify income sources and expenses. A line item budget, together with the auditor's report required by Canon 1.7, is evidence of financial responsibility by the vestry.

10. Vision Statement. A congregation's statement of the vision of what God is calling them to become. A focus toward which to strive. The Vision Statement may be developed periodically—or be carved in granite. It can be a theme for promotional purposes and should be short and memorable ("To know Christ and to love Him").

11. Mission Statement. An articulation of the hopes and dreams of the people of the church who are seeking to be servants of God. Scripture, reason, and tradition help us determine our concept of mission. The dynamics of leadership in the local congregation define how the congregation lives up to its mission. Mission Statements should not be "carved in stone," but rather revisited every 3–5 years.

12. Mission Imperatives. Programs mandated by the Mission Statement. Articulating the mission imperatives adds clarity to the mission statement and identifies how the mission is intended to be accomplished. A common understanding of imperatives developed in the 1970s was Service, Worship, Education, Evangelism, and Pastoral Care (SWEEP). Every ministry program in the life of the congregation should serve one of the mission imperatives. Aligning ministry programs with the mission imperatives provides clarity on organizing the budget to serve the mission statement and on reporting in a Parish Narrative.

13. Planned Giving. This is the method that many use to make their last gift to God through the church out of their accumulated estate after they no longer have need of it. At a basic level it means writing a will and including the church. But it may also include a gift of stocks, bonds or real estate made in a way that provides immediate tax benefits while making a gift. Planned Giving is one of the ways, along with Annual Giving and Capital Giving that God's mission is funded.

14. Pledge Card or Commitment Card (or Estimate of Giving). This is the device used by most people to identify what they intend to return to God for a year's worth of mission. The focus of most Commitment Programs is to receive pledge cards. It is important to remember that, more than the pledge card or the amount pledged, the real purpose of financial commitment programs is to win souls for Jesus. Pledge cards are also known as Commitment Cards (and in some cases, Estimates of Giving). At the deepest level of meaning a pledge card is a signed document saying "I claim Jesus Christ as my Savior. I submit my life to His Lordship." This claiming and submission is signified by a financial commitment which enables the leaders to plan. At a less significant level, but still an important level, it is an act of kindness to the Treasurer. Some cultures do not like pledge cards as they feel that is a debt that contradicts the sense of joyful giving. Other economic situations, such as farming, resist the pledge because income is unpredictable. On balance, no better general way of making a commitment has been determined.

15. Pledging Unit. This refers to a source of a pledge or commitment. It may be an individual or a household. It is useful to think of pledging units when planning a Commitment Program. It helps to determine how many calls will need to be made or letters to be sent.

16. Proportional Giving. This is a way of giving that begins with the question, "How has God blessed me?" rather than "What does the church need?" Then the decision is made to return a proportion or percentage to God in obedience and gratitude.

17. Tithe. The tenth. It is referred to 67 times in the Bible. It is a proportion or percentage. The Episcopal Church has said it is the minimum standard for Christian giving.

18. Stewardship Ministry Team. Every congregation is best served if 4 to 11 people serve as a Stewardship Ministry team who accept the responsibility for Year-Round Education and the Annual Commitment Program.

19. Vestry Stewardship Statement. The Vestry Stewardship Statement is a corporate statement developed and signed by the vestry and clergy. It is a statement patterned after General Convention Resolutions A164 in 1988, A138s in 1997, and A106 in 2000. The Vestry Stewardship Statement, best developed in a retreat environment, completes the following phrases to which all who participate can agree:

> We believe...
> In response to what we believe, we commit... and,
> We call on all members of... to join us...

Essentially this is the leadership's way of saying "join us" rather than "you ought to."

The essential ingredients of a Stewardship Statement include the following:

> We believe... (a statement that witnesses to the collective beliefs of those writing the statement)
> We commit... (a statement that witnesses to the level of commitment in time, talent, and money pledged by the vestry and clergy)
> We commend... (or we invite)... (an invitation to those in the congregation to join the leadership in making a similar commitment)
> (Optional—We Commission... the Stewardship Commission/Committee to...)
> Signatures of Clergy and Vestry members witness to the adoption of the statement.

20. Witness. An essential part of any Stewardship Education or Commitment Program is the sharing of personal stories. The most effective form of witnessing is some version of "I believe..., in response to what I believe, I..., this behavior has impacted my life by..., I invite you to join me." Witnessing is offering an example to be followed by others. Albert Schweitzer is recorded as saying: "Example is not the main thing in influencing others. It is the only thing."

"An essential part of any Stewardship Education or Commitment Program is the sharing of personal stories."

13

The Stewardship Ministry Team

Beginning with the creation of a ministry team for the oversight of all matters relating to resource development is one possible way to begin to effect change in the culture of the congregation. And, the resources to be developed include human (volunteer) resources as well as financial ones.

Many congregations struggle with sustaining the development of both human and financial resources. One congregation may have a finance committee which shapes annual budget requirements and perhaps is even responsible for managing investments. The parish treasurer is often a member. Occasionally this finance committee will even develop a 3–5 year budget plan for the vestry and advise on potential upcoming capital campaign needs. In this congregation a separate organization may be responsible for the annual financial commitment program. This separate stewardship committee is often comprised of new individuals each year.

Another congregation may contain a well-organized small group focused on organizing and running the annual commitment program (Every Member Canvass or Annual Appeal) with little or no connection to year-round stewardship education programs. Such a stewardship ministry team may not have a life beyond the current annual appeal. In this congregation, development and oversight of any multi-year financial plans is likely to be limited to the occasion when the vestry considers it.

If one of these scenarios or some aspects of each resembles your congregation, consider the possibility of combining management of all resource development activities in the congregation under the leadership of a single Stewardship Ministry Team. This ministry team can be charged with the responsibility of oversight for the development and coordination of:

- Year-Round stewardship education programs;
- Hospitality for visitors and newcomers (including commitment programs for volunteer ministry opportunities—time and talent);
- Commitment programs for annual financial giving;
- Programs for planned (or legacy) giving (including policies and administration related to memorials and endowments); and
- Vision planning to consider "what will our congregation look like in 5–7 years, and what must we do now to be ready for it?"

Membership on the Ministry Team should also include leadership of any capital giving program when the life cycle of the congregation dictates. In congregations that have a staff position for volunteer ministry coordination, this individual should be included. The volunteer coordinator will be very familiar with the climate in the congregation and the program opportunities that enable the growth of spirituality and the level of commitment within the membership. The formation process for the team is critical. It is easy to want to begin with identification of many tasks to complete. This is the wrong thing to do! Begin by setting aside as many meetings as it takes to provide for a process of learning to be comfortable with beginning each meeting with Inductive

Bible Study and having each person share their stewardship story in the context of sharing their faith journey. Only after completing this process of formation, should there be any attempt made to share dreams for the future of the congregation, or to begin to analyze where to begin.

Suggested duties of all members:

- Attend regularly scheduled meetings
- Pray regularly (both individually and collectively) for the ministry of each member and for the collective ministry of the team
- Practice tithing (or have a personal plan to be tithing within three years)
- Offer personal and corporate witness to beliefs and practices of financial stewardship, encouraging the vestry and all parish leadership groups to do likewise
- Develop and propose an annual theme for the focus of all ministry programs in the congregation and identify appropriate year-round education and commitment programs.
- Seek vestry approval and funding for the annual plans.
- Collaborate in identifying and recruiting persons to serve in the various programs under the committee's oversight
- Collaborate in identifying outsiders required for consultation, training or presentations
- Develop, for the vestry's approval, a purpose statement (mission statement) for the Ministry Team and include goals for achieving same
- Develop, for the vestry's approval, both the annual and long-range (3–5 year) budget plans (for the Ministry Team) as well as the plans for year-round education, annual giving, capital giving, and planned giving programs
- Be responsible for completing assigned sub-committee responsibilities, individually and in collaboration with others

The function of this Stewardship Ministry Team can be as broad as you want to make it. It can be limited to recommending policy and/or offering guidance, or can be a group that actually stages their own programs. My vision is that it would best function as a point of communication and coordination for all matters relating to the development of human and financial resources.

One congregation that has taken the suggestion of creating a Stewardship Ministry Team seriously has included their outreach ministries programs. One group is responsible for identifying one local outreach program each year that offers the members of the congregation an opportunity for hands-on ministry, as well as financial commitment. Another group is responsible for identifying one global outreach program each year that also offers the members of the congregation an opportunity for hands-on ministry, as well as financial commitment.

Diagnosing the Congregation

Once the Stewardship Ministry Team is created and formed there can be meaningful work done on diagnosing the congregation and creating a plan to effect change. One of the best resources for diagnosing the congregation is the following table which was developed by The Rev. William A. Yon (of Alabama) who was instrumental in the creation of what is known as the "Alabama Plan" in the Episcopal Church.

Conditions Which Constitute OBSTACLES To Effective Stewardship Education In The Congregation	Conditions Which Facilitate EFFECTIVE Stewardship Education In The Congregation
1a. The priest has not made a clear decision about his/her own giving.	1a. The priest is a tither or is committed to a plan of increased proportionate giving with tithing as a minimum goal.
1b. The priest is conflicted about his/her role in leading the parish into more generous giving.	1b. The priest is willing to witness publicly to his/her own understanding and practice of financial Christian stewardship and to invite parishioners to re-examine their own.
2. Vestry members have not made a clear commitment personally to proportionate giving and as a result give mixed signals to the parish.	2. Vestry members are committed to proportionate giving as the pattern of their own financial Christian stewardship and give clear encouragement to their fellow parishioners to do the same.
3. Stewardship messages focus primarily on budget needs and church expenses.	3. Stewardship education focuses primarily on the decision of individual members to give a percentage of their income; budget considerations should be secondary.

Conditions Which Constitute OBSTACLES To Effective Stewardship Education In The Congregation	Conditions Which Facilitate EFFECTIVE Stewardship Education In The Congregation
4. There is little sense of an expanding mission vision to which parish leaders are committed which would require or justify increased contributions.	4. The Rector and Vestry are formally committed to increasing the percentage of parish income devoted to mission outside of the parish, and boldly hold up these specific mission opportunities in front of the congregation.
5. Parishioners are left in isolation to make their own decisions about giving without guidance and support from their fellow Christians.	5. Opportunities are provided annually for parishioners to talk through their decisions about giving with their fellow Christians.
6. Parishioners are sent out to ask for pledges from other parishioners without adequate understanding and skill for this task.	6. Before members visit other members they are given the training necessary to approach this task with clarity and confidence.
7. Stewardship development plans are haphazard and poorly thought out.	7. A careful plan is developed to carry a stewardship education effort through to a successful conclusion.
8. There is little improvement from year to year in a parish's ability to carry on effective stewardship education.	8. Careful evaluation at the conclusion of the program enables a parish to build on successes and benefit from mistakes from year to year.

Use this chart to begin diagnosing the needs of your congregation and develop a plan to move from conditions which constitute obstacles to conditions which facilitate effective stewardship education in the congregation.

Leadership Must Lead

I'm not sure when I first learned the principle that leadership has a responsibility to lead, but I do know this reality: when leadership doesn't lead, the group depending on leadership doesn't make progress. This is an essential truth for us as we encourage generosity for the purpose of doing God's work in the world.

In matters of generosity—and of Christian Stewardship in general—one effective way that leadership can be exercised in congregations is by agreement to produce a leadership stewardship statement (see definition #19).

At first glance, the essential elements of a Stewardship Statement seem simple. Consider, for example, a vestry (or church council) meeting that begins this way:

> "At this meeting we will discuss among ourselves the topics indicated by some open-ended statements. Then we will develop a comprehensive statement on which everyone can agree and bear witness to. It will go like this:
>
> Concerning the subject of Christian Stewardship,
> > We believe...
> > We commit...
> > We invite (or commend)...
>
> Witnessed by (signatures of clergy and each vestry member)"

Without proper preparation and a carefully planned process, chaos may well ensue! The clergy person above will have learned to never approach that subject again!

In a second scenario, vestry members are presented a draft of a completed statement. They are asked to review it, think about it, and maybe even pray about it. In addition, they are to be prepared to discuss the statement, making any necessary minor adjustments, and sign it at the next meeting.

In both illustrations above, the task at hand lacks proper preparation and execution. Paradoxically, the principal benefit of developing a Vestry Stewardship Statement is not in the finished product. Rather it is to be found in the experience of the process itself. There are a number of helpful ways to maximize the opportunities for participants to realize a meaningful experience. A few are:

- Invite a trained facilitator. Look for one who has specific training in the development of stewardship statements.
- Set aside sufficient time for the process. Friday evening through mid-afternoon Saturday is an ideal period.
- Stress the value and importance of participation in the process to the participants. If the expectation is that stewardship be taken seriously by the members of the congregation, then every vestry member must also take it seriously.

- Literally and intentionally recruit every individual vestry member to participate. Do not simply announce when and where the event will take place, leaving the actual attendance of the participants in doubt. Get a commitment to attend.

- Promise the participants a quality experience. Small group Bible study and fellowship are important components of the process.

- Have a plan for sharing the experience with the entire congregation. An article in the parish newsletter (including pictures) can be written by someone who is recruited in advance. The experience can be the subject of the sermon on the Sunday following the event, and the completed statement can be brought forward as part of the Sunday offering. Post the Vestry Stewardship Statement in a prominent place and invite all members to add their signatures of witness. Include the statement on materials developed for distribution during the annual commitment (pledge) program.

A caution: don't carve the statement into stone by engraving it and framing it in a way that suggests, "We did this once, and now we don't ever have to do it again!" Instead, use the statement as a tool in recruiting candidates for election to the vestry. Remind them that an expectation of leadership is to review and renew a witness to a Vestry Stewardship Statement annually. The expectation is that a completely new statement will be developed in the context of a vestry retreat every three years.

Example

> We believe God is the source of all gifts, spiritual and material. Our faithful response, in gratitude, is to be givers and creators ourselves. While we strive to be good stewards of all God's gifts to us, we believe that the way we use our money reflects the state of our spiritual lives.
>
> We commit to follow Christ in community. In prayerful witness to our faith, each of us is already tithing or is committed to increasing his or her personal giving to reach or exceed the tithe.
>
> Our experience is that joyful giving results in spiritual growth. We invite the parish to join us in this commitment to deepening our faith.

Building a Faithful Budget

When building a budget, many congregations look only at contracted expenses—the must-pay items such as electricity, water, disposal, heating, and cooling fees. Frequently the list of must pay items stretches to include salaries and giving to the Diocese (or other adjudicatory).

It is important to start the budget building process in another place. That place is mission. When we speak of mission of the Church, or when we say stewardship is about mission, what do we mean? What is mission? The answer is quite simple: mission is what God calls us to do.

If mission is what God calls us to do, ministry is a way of answering that call. Our ministry is the particular way we respond to God's call. Each person's particular personality, background and circumstances influence his or her ministry. This is also true for the ministry of the local congregation.

A Mission Statement is the place to start building the budget. The mission statement is an answer to the question: "What is Christ calling this community of faith in our diocese (judicatory) to do now?" It is a tool to evaluate congregational activities. It is also a tool for guiding and shaping the parish/mission budget. It helps the members to determine if the budget is a faithful use of the resources that God's people have offered for God's work. The clergy and vestry must lead in the development of the mission statement but should involve all interested members of the congregation. They should encourage members to tell why they have chosen to join this particular congregation. The membership will offer their leaders important understandings of what it believes God is calling the congregation to do. The common themes which emerge will shape the statement.

Once a Mission Statement and Mission Imperatives for a congregation are in place, the budget will unfold in ways that are consistent with the Mission Statement. The process of unfolding can look something like this (or some other way that looks at everything):First evaluate all current expenses in light of the mission statement. How is the mission statement served by line-items in the current budget?

An effective way to make these evaluations is to involve many people, particularly those who work in the parish programs of ministry. All interested members should have a chance to participate.

Each staff person and volunteer ministry group should define his or her ministry by describing or telling how it contributes to the congregation's mission. How are the gifts of time and talent used to further the mission statement? The people involved show how their ministry program will further this mission in the coming year. The mission statement becomes the standard by which all church activities are evaluated.

This process may call for redefining job descriptions. Participants should challenge programming that does not seem to contribute to mission. The goal is to make the budget a witness to the mission statement. For example, from a mission statement's commitment to serving Christ in all persons, the congregation might see an acute need for service to the homeless, or to the elderly, or to some other group. It might then define service to these people as a mission priority. This would make that ministry a budget priority.

1 **A WARNING:** If the Mission Statement is more than 3 or 4 years old, it may need to be revised to make certain that it is still on target.

2 **A SECOND WARNING:** If a congregation does not have a highly visible Mission Statement, any growth in offerings of time or money is unlikely.

People put their money, time and energy into places where they can see it makes a difference. In short, people who give proportionally or tithe, or give beyond the tithe, give because they feel strongly about what is done with the money, time, and energy. They want to know that their giving saves lives or changes them in a positive direction toward God. They give to God for God's purposes. And they will give to God. Whether or not they give to a congregation depends on whether or not they see and hear that the congregation is doing God's work.

3 **A THIRD WARNING:** A Mission Statement that does not have local applications obvious in the text of the statement is not a mission statement; it is a pious hope.

Pious hopes (pious platitudes) are important and useful. But they are not helpful in building a budget. For example, the statement "knowing Christ and making Him known" is a wonderful, pious statement, but it does not answer questions like where, with whom, and when?

4 **A FOURTH WARNING:** Outreach must come first. People who are generous want their congregation to be generous. A simple way to express this generosity is to start with diocesan support. That giving, even though it may be guided by Canon, is outreach giving.

The 1985 General Convention meeting in Anaheim, CA, passed a resolution that encouraged the acceptance by congregations and dioceses of the practice of giving to others as much as we spend on ourselves. The 1988 General Convention passed a resolution (D144s) that encouraged each diocese and congregation of this Church "to continue to work towards the goal of giving to others as much as they spend on themselves (commonly known as 50/50 giving), with at least 25% of the Net Disposable Budgeted Income (NDBI) of each congregation to be given through the diocese for mission and ministry." [NDBI, although no longer used on the parochial report form, is now referred to as "Net Operating Revenue."]

"People put their money, time and energy into places where they can see it makes a difference."

21

At the 1991 General Convention in Phoenix, AZ, 50/50 giving was addressed more strongly.

> *Resolved*, The House of Deputies concurring, That the 70th General Convention of the Episcopal Church in the United States of America affirm that among the many gifts bestowed upon us by a loving God, the gift of the Gospel be seen as central by all baptized persons; and be it further

> *Resolved*, That, as we enter the Decade of Evangelism, we affirm that stewardship of the Gospel is the theological motivation for 50/50 giving, and be it further

> *Resolved*, That the Executive Council be requested to develop resource material which will relate 50/50 giving and the Decade of Evangelism.

This was reaffirmed in the 1994 General Convention held in Indianapolis, IN.

The approach to mission called 50/50 giving testifies to our commitment to mission and ministry beyond the doors of our own local congregation. The 50/50 principle is not a mathematical approach to financial management. Rather, it is a way to put an attitude into practice by adopting a clear, measurable goal. It is a way of enlarging the ministry of our local congregation by committing to financial partnership with other Christian bodies.

50/50 giving is grounded in the summary of the Law,... love your neighbor,.. love yourself... Jesus likewise made reference to this as reported in Luke 3:10-11 "...Whoever has two coats must share with anyone who has none;..."

And, don't forget giving for the future. Give 1% of income to the Seminary or School for Ministry of your choice as part of the 50% given for God's work in the world beyond the parish (congregation).

5 A FIFTH WARNING: Use income from endowment for outreach whenever possible. Congregations that receive substantial proportions of operating income from endowment must work much harder at Stewardship Education. Reliance on endowment income for annual expense tends to create dependency. Dependency is a barrier to growth.

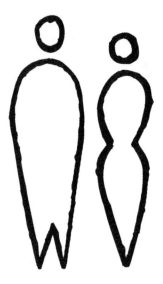

It is impossible to think about Christian Stewardship in any faithful manner without engaging Holy Scripture. The following overview is not exhaustive. It presents some themes with texts identified that are available for study. These passages should be used not as proof texts but as triggers for the interior witness of the Spirit in our hearts.

God the Creator of all	Genesis 1:1-2:24
God's creation is good	Genesis 1:12, Genesis 1:18, Genesis 1:24
We are made in God's image	Genesis 1:27
God is a loving giver	John 3:16
God has given us dominion over creation	Genesis 1:28-31
God makes us Stewards of creation	Genesis 2:15
God accepts our best as offering	Genesis 4:1-4
God gives us children and work	Genesis 3:16-19

Attitude:

Matthew 7:12	I Corinthians 16:13-14	James 1:16-25
John 1:6-18	II Corinthians 4:17-18	James 1:26-27
John 14:1-14	Hebrews 10:24-25	I Peter 1:17-25
I Corinthians 13:1-3	Hebrews 13:16	I John 2:15-17
		II John 1:4-6

What Is Christian Giving?

Matthew 5:23-24	Luke 6:38	I Corinthians 13:3
		I Corinthians 16:2

What Does Jesus Say about Your Money?

Matthew 6:19-21	Matthew 25:14-30

What Is the Kingdom of Heaven Like?

Matthew 13:24-30	Luke 11:5-18	Luke 14:15-24
Matthew 13:44-46	Luke 12:42-48	Luke 16:13
Matthew 5:14-46	Luke 13:6-9	Luke 19:12-27

Danger Signs:

Malachi 3:8-9	Luke 12:10	I Corinthians 1:18-24
Malachi 4:1	Luke 21:34-36	I Corinthians 3:18-20
Luke 3:9	John 3:32-36	Titus 1:13-14
Luke 11:23	Acts 8:20-21	Hebrews 10:29-31
Luke 11:37-54	Romans 1:18-27	Ephesians 4:17-24
Luke 12:8-9	Romans 2:17-34	

Tithing:

Genesis 28:22	Deuteronomy 14:22	Tobit 4:8
Leviticus 27:30-32	Malachi 3:10	Hebrews 7:4

Why Give?

Proverbs 3:10	II Corinthians 8:12-15	Hebrews 13:16
Luke 6:37-38	Ephesians 4:32	James 2:14-17
I Corinthians 4:8	I Timothy 4:8-10	Jude 1:3-4
II Corinthians 9:6-7	Hebrews 10:19-25	

What to Do?

I Samuel 4:9	II Corinthians 9:6-7	II Thessalonians 2:11-13
Matthew 5:23-24	Philippians 2:13	I Peter 4:10
Romans 12:2	I Thessalonians 5:19-22	I John 3:21-24

Why Are You Anxious?

Matthew 6:25-34	Hebrews 12:5-13	I Peter 3:13

Why Should There Be Dissension?

Luke 12:49-53	I Corinthians 11:17-22	Hebrews 10:24-25

Why Tell Anyone My Intention?

Matthew 10:32-33	Romans 2:15-16	II Corinthians 1:12
Luke 12:1-3	Romans 9:1	II Corinthians 12:5
Luke 12:8-9	Romans 14:11-12	Philippians 4:5
Acts 20:25	I Corinthians 1:10	I John 4:1-3
		I John 4:14-16

The Wise, Mature Christian:

Proverbs 16:16	Matthew 7:24	Romans 12:9-16
Matthew 5:3	Luke 11:4-5	II Timothy 3:14
Matthew 5:10-16	Romans 8:9	I John 5:1-5

How Is Your Faith?

Matthew 6:31-32	Acts 15:10-11	Galatians 2:15-16
Matthew 11:25	Acts 16:31	Ephesians 6:13-18
Matthew 17:19-20	Acts 26:18	Colossians 2:6-8
Mark 9:23	Romans 1:6-17	I Timothy 1:18-20
John 6:40	Romans 5:1-5	I Timothy 6:11-14
John 20:3	II Corinthians 16:13-24	Hebrews 11
Acts 6:5	II Corinthians 13:5-9	I John 5:1-5

God Rewards the Giver:

Proverbs 3:9-10	Luke 6:38	II Corinthians 9:10
Proverbs 16:20	Luke 11:11-13	I Thessalonians 5:23-24
Malachi 3:10	Luke 12:8-9	II Thessalonians 3:3-5
Matthew 25:14-30	Acts 20:35	

Why Give Weekly?

I Corinthians 4:1-2	Luke 10:37-42	II Thessalonians 1:11
I Corinthians 16:2	Luke 15:19	I Timothy 1:15-16

Who Is a Good Steward?

Luke 10:38-42   Ephesians 4:17-18   I Thessalonians 2:12
Ephesians 4:1   Colossians 1:9-12   I Timothy 4:8
Hebrews 12:5-6

Why Should the Visitor Turn Down an Unworthy Gift?

Luke 15:19   Ephesians 4:17-18   I Thessalonians 2:12
Ephesians 4:1   Colossians 1:9-12   I Timothy 4:8
Hebrews 12:5-6

Resources Beyond Measure:

Luke 11:5-10   Luke 21:19

Parables about Stewardship:

Matthew 13:1-9   Luke 5:34-38   Luke 14:25-35
Matthew 13:44-45   Luke 7:31-35   Luke 15:1-10
Matthew 20:1-16   Luke 10:25-37   Luke 15:11-32
Matthew 21:33-41   Luke 11:1-10   Luke 16:1-8
Matthew 25:14-30   Luke 12:13-21

Then pray as our Lord teaches us to pray.
Matthew 6:5-13

Inductive Bible Study

A Key to Personal Transformation

Inductive Bible study allows the text of Holy Scripture and the reader to interact at a personal, heartfelt, individual level.

It is simple.

It requires:

- A text from Holy Scripture
- Questions that invite reflection
- Time for reflection
- An opportunity to share the reflection in a non–threatening environment
- An opportunity to pray, grow and determine implications for action

Following are four Inductive Bible studies. Other examples are provided in each of the Commitment Program Workbooks. This method can be applied to any text. These are best done in groups of 4–7 people.

When doing Inductive Bible Study in educational training events, it is suggested that you use a trained outside facilitator who will witness to their stewardship beliefs and practices.

Permission is granted to persons who have purchased this manual to reproduce the Inductive Bible Studies on pages 27-30 for use in the their congregations.

II Corinthians 9:7

"Each of you must give as you have made up your own mind, not reluctantly or under compulsion, for God loves a cheerful giver." (NRSV)

Read the passage aloud together. After a time for quiet reflection, share your thoughts within your study group on these questions.

1. Most of us are reluctant to give because:

    A. (e.g. *"I will not have enough"*)

    B.

    C.

    D.

    E.

These fears (or reasons for being reluctant) are real: *Share with one another the realities of these fears in your life.*

2. Most of us experience compulsion to give:

    A. (e.g. *"I feel guilty when I see poverty"*)

    B.

    C.

    D.

    E.

These compulsions are real: *Share with one another the realities of these compulsions in your life.*

3. If the answer to my fears or reluctance to give is God's ever-loving care providing everything I need, what do I really believe about God's ever-loving care? How do I live this out in my life?

4. If freedom from giving under compulsion comes from knowing God's grace and the fact that God loves me no matter whether I give or not, what do I believe about God's love and forgiveness for me? How do I live this out in my life?

5. How might my life be different if I really could make up my own mind without reluctance or compulsion?

6. How would my giving be different if I could make up my own mind without reluctance or compulsion?

7. What am I going to do about my giving?

1 Corinthians 12:4-12

4"Now there are varieties of gifts, but the same Spirit; 5and there are varieties of services, but the same Lord; 6and there are varieties of activities, but it is the same God who activates all of them in everyone. 7To each is given the manifestation of the Spirit for the common good. 8To one is given through the Spirit the utterance of wisdom, and to another the utterance of knowledge according to the same Spirit, 9to another faith by the same Spirit, to another gifts of healing by the one Spirit, 10to another the working of miracles, to another prophecy, to another the discernment of spirits, to another various kinds of tongues, to another the interpretation of tongues. 11All these are activated by one and the same Spirit, who allots to each one individually just as the Spirit chooses. 12For just as the body is one and has many members, and all the members of the body, though many, are one body, so it is with Christ." (NRSV)

Listen to the passage read aloud. After a time for quiet reflection, share your thoughts on these questions.

1. Note the use of the word varieties in Verse 4. In what spheres of life do these varieties occur? *Share the thoughts.*

2. Note the repetition of the words same and one. Why do you think the author repeats these words so many times? *Share the thoughts.*

3. What does the author say about why the varieties of gifts, services, and activities are given? *Share the thoughts.*

4 How do these verses challenge your view of yourself and your daily life and relationships? *Share the thoughts.*

5. How is this text realized in your congregation? *Share the thoughts.*

6. Spend some time in silence and prayer allowing your mind to roam where it will with this text as a companion.

7. Identify one issue for either yourself or your congregation that you can share with your group in prayer, asking that others join you.

8. Pray together.

BIBLE STUDY

Colossians 3:12-17

[12]*As God's chosen ones, holy and beloved, clothe yourselves with compassion, kindness, humility, meekness and patience.* [13]*Bear with one another and, if anyone has a complaint against another, forgive each other; just as the Lord has forgiven you, so you also must forgive.* [14]*Above all, clothe yourselves with love, which binds everything together in perfect harmony.* [15]*And let the peace of Christ rule in your hearts, to which indeed you were called in the one body. And be thankful.* [16]*Let the word of Christ dwell in you richly; teach and admonish one another in all wisdom; and with gratitude in your hearts sing psalms, hymns, and spiritual songs to God.* [17]*And whatever you do, in word or deed, do everything in the name of the Lord Jesus, giving thanks to God the Father through him.* (NRSV)

Listen to the passage read aloud. After a time of quiet for reflection, share your thoughts on these questions:

1. List some of the things the receivers of the letter were to do.

    a.

    b.

    c.

    d.

    e.

    f.

    g.

2. What was their motivation for these behaviors?

3. What would the church be like if all believers lived up to this model?

4. How can we as individuals support each other as we all respond to these exhortations?

5. Identify one action that you can take. Share it with the group and ask for their prayers.

Jeremiah 31:31-34

As you begin this exercise, explain that the group is asked to please listen (follow along) while the text is read and then, after a period of quiet reflection, be prepared to share what word, phrase or image in the text jumped out at you and some of the reasons you think it jumped out at you.

Someone reads aloud:

31 *"The days are surely coming, says the LORD, when I will make a new covenant with the house of Israel and the house of Judah.* 32 *It will not be like the covenant that I made with their ancestors when I took them by the hand to bring them out of the land of Egypt—a covenant that they broke, though I was their husband says the LORD.* 33 *But this is the covenant that I will make with the house of Israel after those days, says the LORD: I will put my law within them, and I will write it on their hearts; and I will be their God, and they shall be my people.* 34 *No longer shall they teach one another, or say to each other, "Know the LORD," for they shall all know me, from the least of them to the greatest, says the LORD; for I will forgive their iniquity, and remember their sin no more."* (NRSV)

After some quiet time, go around the group asking each person to share what jumped out at them. Do this while thanking each for their response and with no comment from others in the group.

Announce that you will have a second person again read the same text. And then, after some quiet time, we will ask each member of the group to share what troubles you about the text. Do this while thanking each for their response and with no comment from others in the group.

Announce that you will now have a third person read the text. Then, after some quiet time, we will ask each member of the group to share "what do you intend to do about any insights you have gained in this reflection today?" Do this while thanking each for their response, but not forcing any to respond if they choose not to.

After this sharing, the facilitator is to pray for each person by name for empowerment, or ask each person in the group to take turns praying for empowerment for the person on his or her right.

How we have come to know what we know about God and how we feel about the Church has a very significant effect in our financial giving practices.

Stewardship isn't the Episcopal word for fund-raising. The steward is one who is called on to manage something that belongs to someone else. That means two things: First, it isn't really ours, and second, ours is a position of trust and responsibility for that for which we are called to care.

How we know that it really isn't ours is grounded in how we know God. The way we carry out the trust and responsibility for what we have been called to care for is grounded in how we feel about the church.

Stewardship, the word, comes from the Old English term sty-ward and reflects the practice of appointing particularly reliable workers to be wardens of the pig sty; thus, sty-wards. These wardens, living under the word, or the direction, of the lord of the manor, were to become trustworthy custodians of those resources that were indispensable to the life and well-being of the whole community. *They were to lovingly and prudently care for that over which they had authority.*

When the ancient scriptures were being translated, the biblical Greek word *oikonomia* was translated as stewardship. *It was perhaps an act of inspiration that brought the scholars to adopt this term. For it connects the several motifs for an understanding of the gospel and responsible living in community:*

> That is, all persons are to become stewards, servants of God. We are to become persons with responsibility, that is with an office, having authority in the communal life. We are responsible for the physical resources necessary for existence, and we are expected to be diligent in the very earthy tasks assigned in the world, for the very fate of the community depends on our trustworthy custodianship.[1]

This is our understanding of being God's stewards. We are called on to be stewards of each other. Sometimes we are called to be students and sometimes mentors. We each have a role to play in our family in Christ.

This is where all ministry starts: we reach out to others. We reach out to support each other. Sometimes we reach out to be supported. This is something we all are called to do every day of our lives. A smile, a word spoken in a moment of need, a hug when we feel alone.

We all do this, and we probably don't always realize it. That is what being family is.

How we come to know what we know about God is important to our strategies for programs in the church. For our purposes, we are looking at how we have come to know God and the Church. We have discovered that there are six dominant ways in the church today. There may be more. New ones may appear in the future. Each of us has had a unique experience, yet there are common threads that tie us together and help us to understand each other.

**Identity Issues
That Affect
Giving
Practices**

---

[1] Loosely quoted from *Public Theology and Political Economy*, Stackhouse, p. xiii

The six ways of knowing and being known by God commonly observed in the Episcopal Church are Traditionalist, Anglo-Catholic, Rationalist, Evangelical, Charismatic and Social Activist.

Traditionalist: Faith is formed in childhood. Often this faith development is precognitive, before the age of five. People who are traditionalist will often say that they have always known God and that they cannot identify a moment when God became real for them. They love the old ways and traditions of the church and are sometimes fearful of change. The 1979 BCP, moving the altar away from the wall, and women's ordination have been difficult for many. Often this is true because their understanding of "who God is" and "what the church is" is so intertwined. They are oriented toward pastoral care as an important ministry in the church. **Stewardship education** experiences have often been limited in the past to yearly canvasses or letter campaigns, often very low key and usually **tied to the needs of our church and our budget.** This practice encourages maintenance thinking. This invites giving on an external need basis, rather than an internal response to God. When beginning stewardship education with traditionalists, it is important to affirm their experience and to acknowledge that the education program may be uncomfortable because we are inviting change.

Anglo-Catholic: Faith is grounded in mystery, the sacraments, the experience of worship and church aesthetics. One comes to know God through these things. There is a primary focus on the ministry area of worship, and individual needs are met through the outward and visible signs of the sacraments. There is a high value on the **authority of the church**, and often good stewardship has been mandated by the clergy. More emphasis is needed to reclaim the power of the offering. Bringing the offering forward and placing it on the altar ties God's people and their lives to the Eucharist. We offer ourselves to be consecrated, made holy. This is powerful teaching and a place where stewardship education needs to be more articulate. The difficulty for Anglo-Catholics is the inclination to stay in the external, focused on the aesthetics, forgetting the internal movement of transformation. The sacramental aspects of stewardship have been largely untapped, and this may be an area of terrific opportunity to reclaim authentic symbols for our church.

Rationalist: Faith is discovered in paradox. The faith journey and scholarship are of primary importance. Focus is on education. Many clergy are rationalists, as are many who have rejected fundamentalist churches. Rationalists will often talk about stewardship in terms of freedom (liberation) when they give up control of money. Reflecting on the paradox of in whose service there is perfect freedom, for example, rationalists enjoy finding meaning in the tension between the extremes.

Evangelical: Faith is grounded in the conversion experience. All things are seen through the eyes of conversion. The evangelical can tell you the moment his/her life changed. They take scripture seriously and are obedient to God. Frequently the subject of stewardship is not an issue because, for them, scripture is clear, and they are obedient to the tithe. Evangelism is the primary ministry area to which they are called. They tend to soldier on through life, faithful to the call.

Charismatic: Faith is grounded in the personal experience of the spiritual gifts (often speaking in tongues). There is also a quest for personal identification and affirmation in whom they are in Christ. Focus is on worship and Christian community. They know what they know through the gifts of the Spirit. Generally, charismatics come in two types: overt and covert. Overt charismatics need to be surrounded by other charismatics and tend to join charismatic congregations. Covert charismatics tend to be members of ordinary congregations. They are faithful, generally tithe, and are often leaders. They are usually quiet about their gifts, but there are outward signs. Charismatics take scripture seriously and tend to be good stewards, accepting the tithe as the standard.

Social Activists: The quest for justice is primary. Social activists appear to come in two versions: Either they were injured as children and know that offends God, or they read the Bible and believed it. Social activists focus on service. With regard to stewardship, they are often very generous toward causes, willing to sacrifice comfort for justice.

Below is a summary of the starting points for how we know what we know. Almost all of us will be a mixture of these, but there will be one category underlying and supporting all of the others.

Anglo-Catholic: Faith is grounded in the sacraments, experience of worship, and church aesthetics. Focus is on worship.

Charismatic: Faith is grounded in experiencing the presence and gifts of the Holy Spirit. There is also a quest for personal authority and affirmation. Focus is on worship and personal faith experience.

Rationalist: Faith is discovered in paradox. The faith journey and scholarship are of primary importance. Focus is on education.

Traditionalist: Faith was formed in childhood. They love the old ways and traditions of the church and often find change difficult. Focus is on pastoral care and life in the Christian community.

Social Activist: The quest for justice is primary. Many read the Bible and believe in acting on the principles of biblical social justice.

Evangelical: Faith is grounded in the conversion experience and a personal relationship with God. The Bible is of primary importance. Focus is on evangelism and the disciplined Christian life.

A very important thing to do is serious reflection on the nature of your congregation. Recall the voices heard in conversations concerning what it is about the ministry of the church that is important to the members. If your congregation is strongly traditionalist for example, this has serious implications for the type of stewardship education and commitment program that will be effective.

"A very important thing to do is serious reflection on the nature of your congregation. ...this has serious implications for the type of stewardship education and commitment program that will be effective."

33

Many congregations will be primarily of two of the groups, e.g. the traditionalists and rationalists frequently find themselves together. Your primary approach should be designed to send the Stewardship message or messages that are appropriate to each group.

Give careful consideration to the voices you recruit to communicate with the entire congregation. Even though they are tithers, frequently evangelicals and charismatics are not usually the most effective people in communicating with traditionalists.

Social activists, while essential for mission since they help us to face the brokenness and injustice in the world, are seldom appropriate leaders for a stewardship process, unless they happen to be in a congregation of social activists.

Learn to listen to the voices in the congregation to recognize who may be the most effective communicators for the dominant groups in the parish.

The Episcopal Church is wonderfully diverse and complicated. It makes program decisions, especially stewardship, tough. But it makes our community life rich.

Some think that the Episcopal Church has not done much about stewardship. If we were still in the 1950s and 1960s, that would be true.

But things began to change substantially in the 1970s. This development came from several sources. There was enormous success in raising financial commitments for the Venture In Mission program. And, it would be impossible to overvalue the role of the renewal movements. Our people went to Cursillo and Faith Alive weekends and came out changed in a Godward direction. In the Diocese of Alabama a system or method for facing Stewardship issues in life came into being, and that spread across the church.

General Convention began to talk about and finally pass resolutions concerning stewardship. The 1988 General Convention passed a resolution that affirmed the tithe as the "minimum standard of giving for Episcopalians." In a second resolution, the Convention amended the canons to provide that it shall be a duty of the clergy "to instruct all persons in their charge concerning Christian stewardship." This includes teaching "reverence for the creation and right use of God's gifts," the "generous and consistent offering of time, talent, and treasure for the mission and ministry of the Church at home and abroad," and the "biblical standard of the tithe for financial stewardship (Canon 111.14.2.b)." These resolutions are consistent with the sixth Mission Imperative presented to the 1988 General Convention by the Presiding Bishop and Executive Council. This Imperative calls for us to "act in faithful stewardship in response to the biblical teaching of the right use of God's creation."

The 1991 General Convention reaffirmed the resolution of the 1988 General Convention, urging each household to make a financial pledge through their congregation toward the mission of the Church (1988 statistics indicate that the mean figures of pledging in the church is 57.4% of households); and further resolved that each household be urged to base pledging upon a percent of its income, known as proportional giving, and recognize tithing (10%) as the minimum standard of giving.

This resolution was reaffirmed in 1994 in Indianapolis. General Convention continued to pass resolutions on stewardship theology and practice, proclaiming the tithe as the "minimum standard of giving" in 1997 and 2000. However, the 1994 convention was the last time that anyone rose on the floor of the house to speak against the wording of the resolutions in suggesting that "the tithe, or 10% of income, as the minimum standard of giving."

The General Conventions in 1985, 1988, and 1991 passed resolutions that encourage congregations and dioceses to accept "the practice of giving to others as much as we spend on ourselves" (50/50 giving) as a goal to the church.

One student documented that from 1975–1995 giving to congregations in the Episcopal Church was up 82%, after adjustment for inflation. This happened in a time when our membership diminished by a third. Our story is simple—fewer are giving much more.

The Episcopal Church and Stewardship

Current thinking on the part of most Stewardship leaders at the national and diocesan level is focused on three things:

> *First:* Whatever we do, it must serve congregations.

> *Second:* We will do this by providing educational and commitment program resources.

> *Third:* Whenever possible we believe that a trained stewardship mentor is the best way to serve congregations.

Frequently people ask, "What about time and talent?" People give more than money. Most Episcopalians have more money available for giving than they have time. In the past, the church used volunteer time in lavish ways. With the advent of two-income households, that volunteer time has been diminished. A gift of time is very valuable.

In the future we will make four kinds of offerings to God through the Church:

> **First,** we will continue to give money.
>
> **Second,** time will be even more important as a gift than it has been in the past. These gifts of time will be offered for program and prayer.
>
> **Third,** we will see energy as a real gift. Some congregations are experiencing the joy of projects such as Habitat For Humanity. Work projects over weekends and for brief vacation periods can be expected to flourish.
>
> **Fourth,** skills and disciplines have always been offered, but they will become more important. Instead of hiring a carpenter, congregations can be expected to accept offerings from members to accomplish the ministry of carpentry.

The vestry and stewardship ministry team need an effective tool for showing church members how their giving supports mission. Too often, they have only the church's line-item budget to use for this purpose. Although a line-item budget keeps track of church income and expenses it reveals little about how a congregation's mission—its purpose and goals—is funded. And it reveals little about how our offerings translate into effective mission and ministry that makes a difference in the lives of others.

One possibility for displaying the worth of gifts of time and talent, in addition to money, is a narrative format that identifies the number of volunteer hours given in a year. Congregations that have done this using a narrative process (often referred to as a Parish Narrative, Stewardship Report, or other similar name) have been astounded to see what is actually given in non-monetary ways.

A narrative document that shows how the congregation has been supporting mission will encourage increased giving to the church's work in the coming year. This is because the narrative commonly focuses attention not on dollars and cents but on program and people. It is also useful both for showing how the vestry budgets the congregation's resources for accomplishing the work of the church and for soliciting congregational response.

The church is meant to be labor intensive. Therefore, in the narrative report all the costs should be shown and identified in equivalent dollar amounts so that foundational value is apparent when the church space, volunteer hours, and individuals' life-in-the-church stories are appraised. The number of volunteer hours generated by congregations is astounding. Most members of a congregation are not aware of the worth of the physical space of a church. The value of this space can be calculated on the basis of fair rental cost.

The Various Ways to Give to God

Personal stories of lives changed and hopes fulfilled empower the church. The real value of a dollar spent is the story of a life transformed. Congregations can be amazingly cost effective. When a congregation begins to use a narrative report, it typically is surprised to discover how much of God's work is already being done.

A narrative report will not make a line-item budget unnecessary. Both are effective tools for financial reporting, but each type has its special uses. A line-item budget is most useful for planning and keeping track of income and expenses. The narrative report is best for demonstrating how a congregation's contributions of time, talent, and treasure support the work of the church. It is a wonderful vehicle of accountability to the congregation and for the congregation to God.

Planning for a Year-Round Stewardship Development Program

Every congregation needs a stewardship program that fits its situation. The clergy and vestry should create a special Stewardship Ministry Team (or commission or committee) to design and carry it out.

The Stewardship Ministry Team does not work to produce a program to fund the budget. It develops stewardship teaching opportunities to support the Mission Statement. It presents the theology of stewardship to the congregation's leadership. It works for every member to understand stewardship as a faith response.

In trying to establish a point of beginning, determine if the congregation has a sense of its Mission as expressed in its Mission Statement (if one exists). If the Mission Statement is more than three or four years old, it may be time to begin to discover anew the congregation's sense of God's call.

The development of a current Vestry Stewardship Statement is also an excellent way of beginning to get the leaders to focus on their responsibility to lead and witness to their stewardship beliefs and practices to the entire congregation. Vestry Stewardship Statements can be affirmed by succeeding vestries for up to two years. A Vestry Stewardship Statement should be developed from scratch at least every three years. Often the development of a current Vestry Stewardship Statement results in new insights that affect the design of the Mission Statement.

In carrying out faith development, a Stewardship Ministry Team looks for chances to promote stewardship principles. They also take responsibility for capital funds development and planned giving, keeping both within the context of local diocesan mission and ministry priorities.

A planned giving committee as part of the commission is very important (see BCP, p. 445). The commission should invite people knowledgeable about planned giving to lead the congregation in study. The diocesan office of stewardship/development can often recommend a diverse group of good resource people.

The practice of good stewardship requires constant effort. A Stewardship Ministry Team should educate the congregation about stewardship throughout the year. This year-round approach is necessary for improving stewardship practices. The following pages identify a variety of ideas for activities for promoting year-round stewardship education.

The Rt. Rev. John H. MacNaughton, author of *More Blessed to Give*, and retired Bishop of The Episcopal Diocese of West Texas (San Antonio), identifies, beginning on page 104, several issues about the importance of year-round education for stewardship as follows:

> "…without the support of a broader year-round emphasis, even the very best financial stewardship programs, while maintaining their theological/biblical appearance, will over the years degenerate into simple fund raising…. In its broadest terms, what is the heart of our stewardship before God? Is it not to know and to accept that God is the ultimate source of all that we possess…?"

Three Ways to Teach Stewardship Year-Round That Have Some Substance:

1. **Divide the 12 month calendar into four natural stewardship teaching times.**

   a. *January*—Choose a Sunday as near to the first of the year as possible. Here is an ideal time to focus on the theme of the stewardship of time. How do we spend our time? How do we break up the time we are given responsibly between service to self, service to others, and service to God?

   b. *May*—Choose a Sunday around Arbor day. The second stewardship emphasis naturally falls here on the theme of the stewardship of the earth (creation). When we plant a seed in the ground we demonstrate our sense of partnership with God. When we set out a garden, plant a tree or a bush, or sow a field of grain we experience an example of our dependence on the generosity of God expressed through the created order. Spring is an excellent time to be reminded of our responsibilities to protect the gift of all creation in order to pass it on to the future as undamaged as possible.

   c. *September*—Choose a Sunday as near as possible to Labor Day. This is a natural occasion to focus on the theme of our stewardship of talent. Consider a theme in terms of the way that our work—our vocations, professions, and jobs—can be used in helping others, directly or indirectly.

   d. *October to early November*—Normally the focus this time of the year is on stewardship of money. However, the financial aspect of our total stewardship no longer stands alone, but becomes a part of a larger concern, a concern that encompasses most, if not all, of our lives.

In addition to the sermon, all other aspects of the worship service, insofar as possible, should be geared to emphasize the Sunday theme. This includes the choice of hymns, anthems, the use of special prayers on the theme, and at least one bulletin announcement directed to the theme.

2. A second way to bring stewardship into the Church's program year-round is to undertake two Every Member Visitations each year. The fall visitation for financial pledges and the spring visitation for pledges of time and talent.

3. Another effective way to keep stewardship on the minds of the congregation year-round is to use the Sunday bulletin and monthly mailings to write about it. The key to this approach is to have breadth and diversity in the messages in order to emphasize that stewardship is what we do, all the time, with everything we have.

Options for Liturgical Stewardship

I. FALL: PENTECOST, ADVENT, CHRISTMAS, EPIPHANY BCP, 856
Stewardship Ministry: Freedom

1. Theology: Out of the Bondage of Mammon
   Scripture: *Luke 18:18-30*
   ■ freedom from money/materialism
   ■ freedom to give

2. Means: Percent of household resources for annual parish budget

3. Program: Fall commitment program—Every member visitation, dinner, etc.

4. Impact: Empowers the person and parish to spread God's Kingdom in the present

II. WINTER: LENT/HOLY WEEK BCP, 445
Stewardship Ministry: Foundation and Future

1. Theology: Temporal life; provision for future, rich toward God
   Scripture: Luke 12:13-20

2. Means: Capital campaign, bequests, memorials, wills, estate planning, long-term care, funeral arrangements

3. Program: Getting our house in order—legal, wills, estates, burial, nursing homes, columbarium, endowment funds and programs

4. Impact: Stewardship of the person and the family. Allows conversation regarding intentional and inspirational endowment stewardship. Specific projects—benefits Kingdom of God now and for generations to come.

III. SPRING: EASTER, PENTECOST BCP, page 855
Stewardship Ministry: Ministry of Laity

1. Theology: Receiving gifts, discovering gifts, sharing gifts
   Scripture: 1 Corinthians 12:4-7

2. Means: Recruit and call members to share their gifts in specific ministries

3. Program: Pillar Sunday, ministry fair, recruitment, Sunday School parties, Vestry committees

4. Impact: Allows for time and talent stewardship; helps organize for the coming year; before-summer census, involves newly confirmed/received

Sample Twelve-Month Stewardship Planning Calendar

■ January (Epiphany)

Appoint Chair and Committee for year-round stewardship.
Develop Stewardship plan and calendar for the year.
Sermon (New Year's Resolution for Stewardship, Gifts for God).
Youth Epiphany Pageant. Follow up the next Sunday with discussion of Gifts for
  God in youth and adult classes.
Financial Planning Seminar.
Monthly newsletter article on finances/stewardship.

■ February (Lent)

Bible passage on stewardship, discussion at vestry meeting.
Lay person speaks on stewardship at all services on one Sunday.
Blood drive (the gift of life).
Youth Pancake Supper, 10% to world relief.
Lenten sermon on stewardship (Stewardship and Discipline). [Move to March,
  depending on the beginning date of Lent.]
Newsletter article on finances/stewardship.

■ March (Lent/Easter)

Stewardship Committee select Chair and Committee for annual financial commitment
  program.
Planned Giving Forum.
Adult Education program: Durable Powers of Attorney for Health Care and for
  Property and Financial Matters (stewardship of ourselves).
Age in Action—celebrate elders.
Special musical program, recognition of talents.
Newsletter article on finances/stewardship.

■ April (Easter)

Development of stewardship statement by vestry.
Celebrate Creation/Earth Day. Parishioners bring flowers to plant on church
  grounds.
Youth and adult classes discuss living in a safe and clean environment—Caring
  for God's World.
Sermon (Tithing and Taxes—What's the Difference?)
Spring Workday/Clean-up of church building and grounds.
Newsletter article on finances/stewardship.

■ May (Pentecost)

Lay person speaks on stewardship at all services on one Sunday.
Discussion of Vestry Stewardship Statement at adult education classes.
Ministry Fair with Every Member Canvass for gifts of time and talent.
Discussion in Church School classes on stewardship of the environment.
Stewardship Committee finalizes plans for fall financial commitment program.
Newsletter article on finances/stewardship.

■ June (Pentecost)

Mid-year Vestry Planning Retreat. Discussion of Bible passage on stewardship;
  review plans of Stewardship Committee for financial commitment program.
Youth Sunday—recognition for special work/attendance (stewardship of time and talent);
  recognition of teachers.

Blood drive (the gift of life).
Parish picnic. Pie/cake auction with money going to outreach project.
Newsletter article on finances/stewardship.

■ July (Pentecost)

Sermon (Stewardship of Time). Planning for work, play, prayer, and devotional reading.
Program on safety in activities (stewardship of our bodies).
Establish a group to work with Senior Gleaners.
Selection/development of materials for financial commitment program.
Newsletter articles on finances/stewardship.

■ August (Pentecost)

Selection of workers (callers) for financial commitment program.
Plan training program for captains and callers.
Art/Crafts/Hobby show by parishioners, including youth (sharing talents).
Adult Education classes—identify and discuss Bible passages where Jesus talks about money.
Newsletter article on finances/stewardship.

■ September (Pentecost)

Training program(s) for financial commitment program workers.
Vestry discussion of article/book/videos/tape on stewardship.
Wills and Estate Planning Workshop.
Adult Education discussion of theological basis for stewardship.
Church School classes discuss lesson on stewardship.
Newsletter article on finances/stewardship.

■ October (Pentecost)

Annual financial commitment program.
Dinner (or other event) to kick off financial commitment program.
Pledge Sunday(s).
Sermon on stewardship.
Lay person speaks on stewardship at all services on one (or more) Sunday(s).
Graphics on display showing current year income and expenses.
Newsletter article on finances/stewardship.

■ November (Pentecost)

Pledge Sunday(s) and continued calling (if program not completed).
Celebration of concluded commitment program.
Parish Thanksgiving dinner with thanks for gifts of creation.
Start a recycling program at church if one not already in existence.
Fall Workday/Clean-up of church buildings and grounds.
Newsletter article on finances/stewardship.

■ December (Advent/Christmas)

Final report on financial commitment program to Stewardship Committee and vestry.
Evaluation of annual financial commitment program.
Bible study in Adult Education and Church School classes on meaning of gifts and giving.
Program on Year-End Giving of appreciated assets, with tax consequences.
Sermon (How Can We be Stewards of the Greatest Christmas Gift of All?)
Newsletter article on finances/stewardship.

Thirty-Seven Suggestions For Year-Round Stewardship Activities

Listed below are examples of activities which can be used in a year-round stewardship program, designed to emphasize aspects of stewardship which are not directly related to the annual financial commitment program. Some are calendar or church season related, and are so noted.

- Sermon on a New Year's Resolution for Stewardship. (January)

- Epiphany Pageant put on by youth group, with a discussion of gifts for God in Youth and Adult Education classes on the following Sunday. (January)

- Photographer in congregation volunteers to take pictures of parish events during the year for display and for a picture collage or slide show at the annual meeting or the stewardship dinner.

- Blood drive.

- Financial Planning Seminar to assist families and individuals with budgeting.

- Wills and Estate Planning Seminar for general financial planning.

- Wills Workshop—instructions for making a will, including a Durable Power of Attorney for Health Care and a Durable General Power of Attorney for Property and Financial Matters.

- Youth Pancake Supper for Shrove Tuesday, with 10% going for world relief or, even better, with 50% going for mission outside the parish. (Shrove Tuesday)

- Celebrate a Creation/Earth Day and discuss living in a safe and clean environment. Parishioners bring flowers to plant on church grounds; plant a tree on the church grounds.

- Planned Giving Forum (if in April, title might be "Life's Other Certainty").

- Sermon (Tithing and Taxes—What's the Difference?). (April)

- Sermon (How Can We Be Stewards of the Greatest Christmas Gift of All?). (December)

- Spring and Fall Workdays in church and on grounds.

- Pentecost Every Member Canvass for gifts of time and talent. Develop a file from which to recruit as needed.

- Evangelism Workshop—how to tell our own Christian stories (stewardship of the Gospel).

- Pentecost Ministry Fair for recruiting volunteers (stewardship of gifts of the Holy Spirit).

- Recognition Sunday to celebrate ministries.

- Family Workshop—Work, Play, and Pray Together.

- Parish picnic and pie/cake auction with proceeds to go to an outreach project.

- Vacation Bible School themes on stewardship.

- Discussion in Youth and Adult Education classes on stewardship of time: planning for work, play, prayer, and devotional reading.

- Program on Stewardship of our bodies—safety in activities, health care plans, balance in daily living.

- Art/Craft/Hobby Show by parishioners, including youth—sharing talents.

- Used clothing collection to be distributed to the needy.

- Workshop on recycling, including how to start a compost pile. Plan effective recycling at church of office paper, bulletins, newspaper, cans, bottles, etc.

- Youth project: recycling to earn funds for a service project.

- Blessing of the Animals. (October 4, St. Francis Day)

- Parish Thanksgiving Dinner, with thanks for the gifts of creation. (November)

- Workshop: Advent Wreaths made for homes, complete with candles, liturgy, and prayers to be used by families (stewardship of Christ's coming—God's gift to the world). (November)

- Bible Study: theology of gifts and giving.

- Gifts for the homeless and for food closets.

- Educational Program on Year-end Giving of Appreciated Assets, with the tax consequences.

- Newsletter article: Include the Church on Your Christmas Gift List! (December)

- Lenten Calendars to remind us of sharing our wealth with the poor. (February, March)

- Youth outreach—assist elders with spring and fall clean-ups at their homes.

- Church birthday party for Pentecost.

- Potluck Supper with international theme—focus on the international community and world-wide church.

Congregational and Individual Issues That Affect the Success of the Commitment Program

An effective commitment program intentionally relates to the decisive factors of success: leadership, context, congregation. That is, the ability and commitment of the leaders, the socio-economic environment of the church and the kind and number of people who make up the membership are the main factors that determine the shape of all successful programs.

It is, therefore, important to spend time diagnosing the current situation of the congregation. What did you do last year and the two or three years prior? What worked, what didn't and why? What are the realities of the congregation now in contrast to how it might have been the prior few years? Things to consider include:

- Are there lots of new members vs. fewer members vs. not much change?
- Is there an upbeat economy vs. anxiety producing economic conditions?
- Is there a new Rector vs. no Rector vs. same Rector as for many past years?
- Is there an energized leadership team vs. leadership exhausted from the latest capital improvement project?
- How is the perceived level of trust of the leadership?
- Is there a sense of vision for the future of the congregation?
- Are we a very large or a very small congregation?
- Are there only a few families (or endowments) who essentially provide the vast majority of the annual operating financial support for the congregation vs. 25–40% of the households that provide at least 80% of the financial support?
- What is the general understanding of the theology of stewardship in the congregation (go out and ask the leadership, don't guess).
- Is the parish in conflict or generally depressed?

All of these things, and more, have an influence on the kind of program that is best suited for the culture of the congregation in any given year. By analysis of the current conditions in the congregation vs. those that are desirable, the leadership will be able to identify, select, and design both the education and commitment programs. For obvious reasons, all of the key leadership of the congregation should be involved in this evaluation.

Perhaps the single most common factor that weakens the stewardship development efforts in a congregation is the tendency to procrastinate. The earlier that dates are set, the program designed, the materials ordered, publicity begun and workers recruited, the more effective the program will be!

The following outline identifies the most common types of commitment programs in the Episcopal Church.

The first five programs are referred to by the titles of the companion workbooks to this manual. The workbooks include a detailed outline guide for the organizing, recruiting, and training components of the program. The recruiting formula identified below for these programs is fully explained in the workbooks. The first number 10 refers to the size of the leadership group (representing 10 different households); the second number 10 refers to 10% of the remaining households (after deducting 10 for the leadership group); the third (and fourth) number are explained with the formulas below.

A. **The Faithful Member Home Visitation Commitment Program (Every Member Canvass)**

Program Description: Visitors are recruited and trained to make personal visits in the homes of the remaining members of the congregation.

Recruiting Formula: 10-10-3-2. The Leadership Team (of 10) identifies members of 10% of the remaining households to recruit to serve as Recruiters (and attend the training event) who, in turn, each recruit three Visitors who agree to attend the training event and visit two households.

The basic requirements for a successful Faithful Member Visitation Program include:

1. Carefully recruited, trained, and motivated Visitors; enough so that no caller (or recruiter) is expected to make more than three calls!
2. A thorough training event, no Visitor visiting without participating in the training.
3. Careful screening of the homes to receive visits. Do not visit where there will be no welcome.
4. A leader to personally report back to after the calls are completed.
5. Mail contact with all households before and after the calls.
6. A celebration to honor the callers and other program leadership.

B. **The Festive Meal (Banquet or Loyalty Dinner) Commitment Program**

Program Description: All energies of the congregation are focused toward one major event. Table Hosts are recruited and trained and assigned members whom they invite to join their dinner table group. Discussion Leaders, who are matched with Table Hosts, are also recruited and trained. In large congregations, it may be necessary to host more than one event, either concurrently or at different times.

Recruiting Formula: 10-10-2. The Leadership Team (of 10) identifies members of 10% of the remaining households to attend the training event and serve as Recruiters who, in turn, each recruit two (from separate households) to attend the training and be a Host or a Discussion Leader.

The elements for a successful Festive Meal Program are:

1. A wonderful place for the meal
2. Good entertainment
3. An inspiring speaker
4. A brief Bible study
5. Recruited and trained table hosts
6. Recruited and trained discussion leaders
7. Mail contact with all households before and after the event.
8. A celebration to honor the table hosts, discussion leaders, and other program leadership

C. **The Personal Note (Direct Mail) Commitment Program**

Program Description: A select group is recruited to write their stewardship witness to use as letters and/or bulletin inserts. Note Writers are recruited to attend a training event and to write short personal notes to the households in the congregation who are not represented at the training.

Recruiting Formula: 10-10-2. The Leadership Team (of 10) identifies and recruits members of 10% of the remaining households to serve as Recruiters who, in turn, each recruit two (from different households) to attend the training event and be a Note Writer.

The elements for a successful Personal Note Program are:

1. Six pieces (minimum) of handwritten mail into each home, such as:
   a. Letter from the Stewardship Program Chair—informs what is going to be done
   b. Letter from the Rector—the Theology statement
   c. Letter from a revered lay person
   d. Letter from a second revered lay person
   e. A hand-written letter from a parishioner that is written at the training event
   f. A Thank-You note also written by the same parishioner at the training event

2. A group that represents not less than 25% of the households in the congregation is recruited to attend a training event where they compose handwritten notes inviting other members of the congregation to join in making a pledge. Thank-you notes also written at the same time.

3. Letters "a–d" are best if handwritten. If that is not feasible, use the very best mail merge program available (possibly a handwriting font) and hand-address and hand-stamp the envelopes.

4. Remember "six schticks" and they must have a personal touch. Your goal is to have parishioners respond. It's imperative that your messages have a creative personal touch (for example, theme stationery, off-size envelopes, etc.).

5. Those who attend the training event receive a thank you letter from the rector after receipt of their pledge.

6. A celebration to honor the recruiters, note writers and other program leadership.

D. The Cottage Meeting Commitment Program

Program Description: Each member of the congregation is invited to attend one of many small group gatherings in the homes of Hosts who have been recruited. Trained Discussion Leaders and Witnesses, who are matched with Hosts, are also recruited and trained.

Recruiting Formula: 10-10-2. The Leadership Team (of 10) identifies and recruits members of 10% of the remaining households to serve as Recruiters who, in turn, each recruit two to attend the training event and to serve as a Host, a Witness or a Discussion Leader. Often Discussion Leaders also serve as Witnesses. Sometimes it is best to separate these roles.

The elements for a successful Cottage Meeting Program are:

1. A host home for every 8–10 persons in the congregation
2. A trained host(ess) for each home
3. A trained discussion leader (and witness) for each home
4. A brief Bible study or other reflection
5. A brief discussion on the vision/ mission of the parish
6. Dessert
7. A celebration to honor the recruiters, hosts, discussion leaders, and other program leadership

E. The Home to Home Commitment Program

Program Description: The homes of the members of the congregation are divided into neighborhoods of 4–5 households, each with a Coordinator. A pledge packet that is assembled at a training event is routed around the neighborhood.

Recruiting Formula: 10-10-2. The Leadership Team (of 10) identifies and recruits members of 10% of the remaining households to serve as Area Recruiters who, in turn, each recruit two to attend training event and to serve as Neighborhood Coordinators.

The elements for a successful Home to Home Commitment Program are:

1. Follow the outline for organization and delivery published in the workbook.
2. Put out a lot of informational publicity about how the system works so that people will understand that it is critically important for them to do their part in keeping the package routed to completion.

3. Have a leadership group that constantly monitors the process to intervene in the slippages and interruptions.

4. Use creativity in assembling the container to be routed from home to home. In the packets that stay with each household, include lots of material about how the congregation is living into its mission, including opportunities for the future. This is an excellent place for including a Parish Narrative.

5. A celebration to honor the recruiters, neighborhood coordinators, and other program leadership.

F. **The Telephone Appeal**

The requirements for a successful telephone appeal include:

1. Do what the professionals do—borrow or rent a phone bank.
2. Script the telephone calls.
3. Train the callers at a training event that includes Inductive Bible Study and the witness of the facilitator.
4. Have the callers all in one large room. Have cheerleaders hustling soft drinks and snacks. Pause from time to time to let the callers tell the stories of their calls.
5. Don't stop until everyone is contacted.

G. **The Patch and Match/Beat-to-Fit Program**

Sometimes it is useful to combine several of the elements of multiple program methods into one.

For example, it is usually helpful to send out six pieces of mail no matter what commitment program method is used.

Some people don't want to be called on in their home—contact them in some other way.

In larger congregations, it may be useful to use a combination of several different commitment program methods. For example, a large downtown congregation utilized a combination of a Cottage Meeting and Festive Meal all in one evening. The home/table hosts invited an assigned group of folks to meet in their homes prior to the evening's Festive Meal. While in the homes at the pre-party, the guests had refreshments and a small group Bible study. Each of the small groups chose their own dinner theme and everyone in each small group brought a dish that contributed to the dinner for their small group. After the pre-party activities, the groups adjourned to the parish hall for an evening of musical entertainment while they enjoyed their dinners. The parish hall was decorated in a festive mood and the variety of theme dinners enjoyed by each table added to the excitement of the evening.

Those who study the dynamics of how mail is received and perceived tell us that the envelope is first reviewed to see if this is a personalized message or just another mass-marketing mailing. Is it any wonder that invitations to important events come in envelopes that truly look important. Personalized addresses (no mailing labels—and preferably hand addressed), colorful first class stamps, and something other than the ordinary stationery of the congregation will most likely invite opening of the envelope. Misspelling the name of the recipient is not well received.

Once the envelope is opened, the recipient will scan the letter to see how their name is spelled, who wrote the letter (is it really signed), and if there is a P.S. message. The P.S. may be the only thing read—it had better invite reading the body of the letter. If the recipient is still comfortable proceeding, they will read the first sentence. It better be a good one with a hook. With no hook, the letter will likely be discarded.

To make your messages effective for the more committed members of your congregation, it is essential to individualize the message with custom verbiage that connects with the individual member. "That's inefficient, and way too much work!" you may say. I agree, it is inefficient and it is a lot of work. Remember, you want your communications to be effective. To be effective, forget about trying to be efficient. Being efficient won't produce communications that connect with the individual hearts of your members—effective communications will. To make it easy for your members to respond, include a return envelope. And, for your most committed members, include first-class postage on the return envelope.

Mailings

A good rule to remember is that *a principal point of having a commitment program is to get at least 25% of the households of the congregation in attendance at an educational training event in order to help grow grateful and generous hearts for the spread of the Kingdom of God*. If, on the other hand, the focus of the program is seen as one to raise money then it may well indeed raise money for that one particular occasion. However, don't expect there to be any permanent conversion of hearts or minds as to why we should give of ourselves for God's work in the world through our local congregation. And, don't expect the commitment program to be any easier the following year!

Organizing for Stewardship Commitment Programs

Success depends on the following factors—include them in whatever program you do:

Pray
- often as a committee
- often as individuals
- often as leaders of the congregation
- for the workers (borrow from Cursillo)

Purpose
- to win souls for Christ
- identify an annual purpose statement (and theme)

Plan
- a program appropriate for the congregation
- create the program plan at least 6 months in advance of the Big Event

---

Recruit
- the Ministry Team to define the annual plan and the master plan for acceptance by the vestry
- competent folks... define the tasks (job description)
- the annual program leadership (this year's Big Deal)

Rally
- around a theme (don't forget anniversaries) appropriate to the life of the congregation

Reward
- those who work in the program (volunteer appreciation)

Ask
- for the pledge commitment

All
- households are informed (contacted) concerning the program plans
- are invited to pledge (don't forget the youth)
- are visited (when visiting) except those who say "no"

Acknowledge
- those who work/lead and pledge (thank you notes)

Involve
- as many folks as possible (break out jobs into small tasks) (efficiency does not equal effectiveness)

Invite
- Include messages of invitation "I invite you to join me in experiencing the mystery, the wonderment, etc."

Start Early
- at least 6 months before the Big Event/Loyalty Sunday

Six "Schticks"
- a minimum of six messages—spaced out... working through the information smog of our culture

---

Education
- include year-round education program activities
- for clergy, vestry and key program leaders (Training Event)
- for all recruited—everyone who will have one on one contact with members must come to the training (make it convenient)

Examples
- Schweitzer: "Example is not the main thing in influencing others, it's the only thing."
- Stewardship Statement of Vestry and Clergy
- Personal witness stories (BEST from peers) (OK—packaged messages) Personal witness of clergy is essential.
- Use both verbal and written
- Ministry stories—examples of how peoples lives are being changed by the ministry of the people of God at "_____" e.g. I want you to know that your offerings enabled _____ to happen this past week.
- Parish Narrative presents/packages a way to raise up examples of God's work.
- Ways that acknowledge "who has."

Epistemology
- We have come to know God in different ways

Evaluate
- understand the giving patterns in the congregation
- the effectiveness of each annual commitment program—document the learnings

Why Recruit?

Why recruit? Why not just take volunteers? The basic answer to these questions is "because that's what Jesus did!" Several biblical references are Mark 1:16-20, Matthew 4:18-22 and Luke 5:1-11. When we just accept volunteers we surrender control of the quality of our work to the whims of people who may or may not be competent and committed and who may not have the gifts required for the work.

It is important to remember how Jesus recruited. He said, "Follow me." He did not do it the way we want to do it. The way we normally want to recruit is contained in the St. Richard of Chichester hymn, *Day by Day*, in *The Hymnal 1982*, page 654. "Day by day, dear Lord, three things of thee I pray: to see thee more clearly, love thee more dearly, follow thee more nearly, day by day." This is a perfectly wonderful way to grow in piety. But it is backwards from the way Jesus recruited. Jesus did not say, "Here is a set of *The Interpreter's Bible*. Read everything until you understand me. Then after you understand me, why don't you think about whether or not you love me. If you love me, then decide to follow me."

No, he recruited and did so by simply saying, "Follow me."

What Kind of Person to Recruit

Normally, we in the church assume that commitment is the key issue in whether or not a person should be asked to help do something. But, the level of commitment does not have the primary role in determining the quality of job that a person will do. Competence does.

There are generally four kinds of constituencies in a congregation. (1) There are competent, committed folks. In the Statistical Church Chart that analyzes the giving patterns of congregations, these are the twenty percent who are leaders. (2) There are committed folks who aren't particularly competent. (3) There are uncommitted folks who exhibit competence in other areas of their lives. (4) There are some folks whose lack of commitment is matched by a fundamental lack of competence. These four constituencies can be charted in a four-part window.

	Competent	Incompetent
Committed	The 20% The Leaders	
Uncommitted		

When we are short of leaders we normally turn to other committed people. But this is not always productive. Instead, we have found that if we recruit competent, but uncommitted, folks and provide them with training, they will grow in commitment to match the task.

How to Recruit

In the church we have too often allowed people to say no without articulating the no, and then we wonder why nothing happens with our dreams and expectations. One of the roles of a consultant may well be to help the group (re)evaluate the myths they live with.

Rules for Success in Recruiting Competent, Committed People:

■ Remember: recruit persons who exhibit competence in the other areas and arenas of their lives.

■ Recruit persons who have demonstrated a sense of commitment by their history of pledging to the parish. When recruiting for leadership positions, it is critical to know you are recruiting seriously committed persons. When recruiting for worker positions, it is important to include a mix of proven competent, committed people together with competent people who may not yet be converted to a deep sense of commitment.

■ Arrange for the visit. When recruiting leaders it is important to make this an important personal visit; perhaps a one-on-one visit for lunch or dinner that has been scheduled by a personal telephone call. When recruiting workers, an advance letter can be used advising them that they will be contacted and requesting their prayerful consideration.

■ Greet the person by name, and touch them. Touching style can vary from a handshake to a hug. Smile! Be sincere! Be organized!

■ Tell them the work is important—"and I know you care about _____ because _____."

■ Tell them the work is hard.

■ Tell them the exact scope of the work.

■ Tell them the work is manageable; they'll get the training they need.

■ Tell them their success will be recognized and rewarded.

Key Skill Issues: Eye Contact; Say Their Name (at the beginning and end); Touch Them; Express Feelings. The following acronym can be useful:

> SOLER: **S**quare off
> **O**pen posture
> **L**ean forward
> **E**ye contact
> **R**elax and be genuine

When Recruiting:

■ Remember that affirmation works—use affirmation techniques in describing the traits needed and then noting "you have those traits" (if indeed they do).

■ Don't twist arms—invite him/her to join you.

■ Define the full scope of the commitment when recruiting. A sample job description follows.

The _____ Commitment Program
(*Customize for your Congregation*)
[Church Name] Stewardship Commitment Program 20__
(*Program Theme, if any*)

Job Description for Recruiters... What you are being asked to do....

You are being asked to provide a very important link to several households in the parish: to recruit people to attend a Stewardship Training Session. This session is a key component of our parish's stewardship program, as it will determine at what level the parish will conduct its ministries to fulfill its mission in 20__.

Recruiting people to participate in this session is also important to the ongoing development of new leadership in our parish.

Here are the specific tasks or activities you are being asked to do:

■ Attend a Training Session.

■ Make your own pledge at the Training Session, or before you begin recruiting.

■ You will invite/recruit ___ people/or couples to sit at your table at the Stewardship Training Session on _____ (specify date). This recruiting will be done face-to-face wherever possible.

■ At that session you will help facilitate group discussion (and any exercises we may do).

■ You will join those you invite in the group exercises.

■ You will write a thank you note to those who attended with you, thanking them for their time and commitment to the parish mission.

■ You will collect and turn in to the Stewardship Committee any pledges collected at your table at the session.

It is important to recruit people face-to-face whenever possible, and to stress that you are asking them to join you in a process you have already experienced and feel is important to the ongoing life of the parish and its mission.

Matching the Person and the Task

It is important to match the right person to the right ministry. The section in this manual on "Identity Issues That Affect Giving Practices" provides tools for assisting in the assessment of our gifts.

Some insights:

> Don't ask an Evangelical to lead a discussion group entitled, "Moral Ambiguity as a Pathway to God." Ask a Rationalist.

> Don't ask a Traditionalist to lead a ministry to ex-convicts living in the community. Ask a Social Activist.

> Analyze any ministry in terms of the "how we have come to know God" spring it flows from. Find someone who drinks from the same spring.

Training Leaders For Stewardship Work

A good consultant can be very helpful. The experienced consultant can be of invaluable assistance in helping to diagnose and analyze the congregation in order to identify the best Stewardship Development Program for a particular time in the life of a congregation. An experienced consultant will know which parts of a particular program are crucial to success and which are optional. She or he knows how to combine the strengths of various programs to create one that is right for a particular congregation.

For assistance in locating a consultant contact the leadership of your diocesan stewardship program to see if your diocese has an established team of trained consultants or resource persons.

Assistance is also available by contacting:

Mr. Tom Gossen
Executive Director
The Episcopal Network for Stewardship
316-686-0470 or 1-800-699-2669
E-mail: tomgossen@tens.com
Internet address: http://tens.org

Essential Elements of Training

1. Use prayer to open and close the sessions.

2. Incorporate Inductive Bible Study with texts that point toward the task or ministry at hand.

3. Witness stories about the how, what, why of the ministry or task. This is the most difficult and perhaps the most important part of the process. Cheerleading doesn't help. Honest stories of the journey and struggle do.

4. Utilize small group processing for everything. One key insight for the participants is the knowledge that they are not alone.

5. Incorporate time for reflection.

6. Invite decision, "Will you…?"

7. Provide refreshments for the body.

Five Tips to Help Your Training Work

1. Start on time

2. Value time

3. End early

4. Be present the whole time

5. Ground Rules:
   - Listen
   - Talk straight
   - Respect other people's ideas, even if you don't agree
   - Come prepared
   - Stay on the topic
   - Encourage creative thinking
   - Recognize that conflict is not necessarily a bad thing
   - Participate
   - Hold everyone to the same rules

Rule of Fours

To ensure success, a minimum of 25% of the parish family (household) units should be involved in the stewardship commitment program as leaders and workers.

For example, for optimum effectiveness in a congregation of 300 household units, there should be a minimum of 75 households represented at the training event and involved in the commitment program as leaders or workers. Structure the program so that no one is expected to make more than four contacts or visits.

Creating a Safe Environment for Training

The following factors can have an impact on the sense of comfort instilled in those that come for the training:

1. Initial impression must communicate, "You are special." Be sure signs clearly and effectively welcome people, provide them directions to meeting rooms and rest rooms, and inform them where to be and at what time.

2. Provide lots of stuff they can pick up, pin on, and carry—agendas, personalized packets, name tags, tables with collateral documents on display, as well as badges for workshop presenters and helpers.

3. Start on time. Set and maintain schedules for a) breaks b) meals c) free time.

Prayer for a Training Session or a Meeting

Lord, Eternal God,
      we are about to begin our training (meeting)
      and we do so with the awareness
      that without Your Divine Presence
      here at the center of our session (meeting)
      and also within ourselves—
      our work will be empty.

Grace us with Your Wisdom and Vision;
      gift us with Holy Humor and Humility
      so that not only this training (meeting)
      but all our lives
      may be a meeting place
      for Your Kingdom.

We ask this through our Lord, Jesus Christ,
      who lives with You
      in the unity of the Holy Spirit,
      now and forever.

Amen

Shantivanam House of Prayer
Easton, Kansas

Training/Educational Opportunities

There are a number of suggested models for training the various leadership groups in a congregation that must become involved over time for there to be an effective Stewardship Development Program. An experienced and trained consultant will be able to discern with the parish leadership what parts of which models are most appropriate for each given situation.

The variety of opportunities can be characterized to include the following:

- Introduction to Stewardship Development Program Theology for clergy, vestry and other parish stewardship program leaders. A 3–4 hour program.
- One day (minimum 6 hr. for first time) or Fri./Sat. overnight retreat to develop a Clergy/Vestry Stewardship Statement.
- One day (minimum 6 hr.) or Fri./Sat. overnight retreat to develop a Mission Statement.
- A 3–6 hour Training program for Congregation Leaders.
- A two-hour workshop to develop a Commitment Program strategy.
- A 3–6 hour event for gathering and discovering parish stories for a Parish Narrative (Narrative Budget).
- A 3–6 hour Training program for Commitment Program Workers (Visitors, Hosts, Note Writers, Telephone Callers, etc.)
- Festive Dinner for all members of the congregation with Bible Study and an inspirational speaker.

At the time that it feels like no more follow-up efforts to seek out commitment cards will be fruitful, it is time to evaluate the effectiveness of the just-completed program. An evaluation should discover what worked and what might have been better if done otherwise in order that those responsible for future programs have the benefit of our learning from the current year. The evaluation process should involve all of those who were actively involved with the program planning and execution. Don't invite conflict by the nature of the evaluation process.

If planning calendars were initially made and kept current during the progress of the program, they can be a useful tool to begin to identify what happened on a timely basis (as planned) and what didn't. Identify these issues in a caring and factual manner to learn for the future, not in any way that will lay guilt on people when things that didn't work are identified.

In addition to evaluating what happened as planned and what could have been more timely (or scheduled differently to be more helpful), it is useful to evaluate the numerical statistics of the pledges in hopes of learning something about how people may be growing in their commitments to God as expressed in their financial commitment. The following kinds of information can be useful.

**Evaluating and
Planning for
Next Year**

Of the pledges that were currently made and also made in the prior year:
- how many (and what percentage) increased the amount of their pledge
- how many decreased their pledge
- how many pledged the same both years

How many new pledges were received?

How many pledges were renewed from years prior to the immediate past year?

A vigorous program of stewardship education and visitation can be expected to awaken others in the congregation to the importance of annual re-examination of their giving practices.

From the increased pledges for the current year, identify how many increased by (a) 1–25%; (b) 26–50%; (c) 51–75%; (d) 76–100%; (e) more than 100%.

All Christians are called to give in proportion to their means. As they change from the habit of dollar-giving to the practice of pledging a percentage of income, pledges can be expected to be increased significantly.

Of those who decreased their pledge, try to determine why. Were the reasons varied? Do they seem reasonable? Is there a pattern?

How many households have not pledged in either of the past two years?

Visitation or other contact with this group prior to the next commitment program may help to clarify their membership status, so that a determination can be made of the appropriateness of including them in the next appeal.

Identify the number of pledges for the current year in $500 increments to determine if a pattern can be identified of the number of families who have not yet adopted a practice of proportionate giving. Generally, the number of pledges below $1,000–$2,000 will be revealing of the significance of how many have not adopted this practice.

Once the above data is analyzed, it is important to pause and pray for a non-judgmental attitude toward those who have not yet given all that they possibly can of their time and their money for God's work in the world. A trained Stewardship Consultant should be able to assist you in designing your program for the next year with the emphasis on the group(s) you wish to try to reach.

Remember, as Albert Schweitzer is quoted as saying:

"Example is not the main thing in influencing others. It is the only thing!"

Workbooks and program supplies are currently available from Morehouse Publishing for the following Commitment Programs:

- The Personal Note Commitment Program
- The Faithful Member Home Visitation Commitment Program (Every Member Canvass)
- The Festive Meal Commitment Program
- The Personal Note Commitment Program
- The Cottage Meeting Commitment Program
- The Home to Home Commitment Program

Other Resources

The Episcopal Network for Stewardship is a voluntary network of people who understand the important role of leadership in calling the Church to a faithful response to God's call to generously share of our time, talents and treasures to provide for God's work in the world.

> Our purpose ...
> to lead in the growth of a network of dedicated stewardship ministers serving congregations and dioceses; and, to support each other with personal consultations and fellowship opportunities, as well as print, video and electronic resources.

For information call 800-699-2669; *Fax* 316-686-9102; *E-mail* tens@tens.org or visit http://tens.org A comprehensive bibliography is kept current on this web site along with dozens of useful links to resources to help with year-round programs.

If you are interested in learning more about Vestry Stewardship Statements, order Resolution A138s is Alive and Growing... from The Episcopal Network for Stewardship by calling 800-699-2669 or 316-686-0470. The cost is $10 plus S/H (US$) for a set of three booklets. Resolution A138s is Alive and Growing... was developed by the Standing Commission on Stewardship and Development as a report to the 2000 General Convention of the Episcopal Church in response to Resolution A138s of the 1997 General Convention. In addition to an outline for the process and many sample Stewardship Statements, this publication includes stories from vestries and diocesan leaders on their experience in developing Stewardship Statements.

The following are available by contacting Morehouse Publishing at 1-800-877-0012:

One Minute Stewardship Sermons by The Rev. Charles Cloughen, Jr. A collection of messages that can be used at the offertory each Sunday, incorporated into the regular sermons, or printed in the bulletin. These "sound bytes" reflect on the many aspects of stewardship that a congregation experiences throughout the year. This is a very practical book, full of information you can use.

Grateful and Generous Hearts by The Rev. Dr. John H. Westerhoff. If you're looking for the single most important resource (in addition to the Bible) to begin using with your newly formed Stewardship Ministry Team, this is the one!

Videos produced by The Episcopal Network for Stewardship in association with "The Friends of the Groom," a professional Christian theater company, and Conover Production Services: The Spiritual Journey Owner's Manual Series. Available in both VHS and DVD format.

The Lord's Prayer: Discover the Secrets of the World's Best-Known Prayer—This professionally produced 10-minute video shows how Linda, a typical casual church-goer, learns to slow down and begin to apply the words of The Lord's Prayer to her life. Guided by the voice of God, the two take part in a give-and-take conversation in which Linda discovers what God wants from her. At the end of their talk, she begins to take the first few tentative steps toward the life she is meant to have... with God's assurance that He will be with her every step of the way. For all ages, but especially meaningful for adults 25–65. A study guide comes with the videotape that is designed to use in groups or for one's individual spiritual journey.

Loose Connections: Tighten up Your Connections with God. In this production, Jocelyn's hectic schedule is cut short by a long, impatient wait at an auto repair shop. She strikes up a conversation with a man named Jesus, whom she assumes works at the shop. They discuss Jocelyn's feelings about going to church—that there are too many expectations of her and a lot of guilt for not tithing—so she attends less and less. Jesus tells Jocelyn that when her son, Frank, prays for her, he merely asks that she know the she is really loved. When she realizes the power of that simple prayer, Jocelyn knows that her heart is ready to lead her back to church. Discussion/study guide included. An essential tool for stewardship education for both adults and youth.

Notes

Notes